ARCHANGELOLOGY MICHAEL PROTECTION

IF YOU CALL THEM THEY WILL COME

KIM CALDWELL

Ꝥ Together Publishing

A Division of Together Publishing http://www.
togetherpublishing.com

Introduction Editing and enhancement Rachel Caldwell

Book Editing Grammarly

ISBN: 978-1-947284-20-3

Book Cover Picture Nicola Zalewski

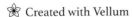 Created with Vellum

ABOUT THE SERIES

"Logic will get you from point A to B. Imagination will take you everywhere."-- Einstein

This piece is one of a series of Angelic Upgrade books that fill you with Divine Angelic codes. Angelic laws are based on love and light thus, operate for free-will, so we must call and ask the Archangels for help.

When working with your book relax, take deep breaths and ground to Mother Earth. Focus on Intentions for whatever it is your heart desires that are for the highest good of all involved. Intentions for these energies that we can not see but feel when we are ready. There are those that believe The Archangels are the Ones that make Law of Attraction Work.

This series of books take on a life of its own as the Archangels move and play from book to book, creating a Delicious Alchemy. Each book becomes an instrument in this Celestial Symphony for a more fulfilling life. Many of the Archangel books also carry and infuse the Violet Flame and Divine Connection to Mother Earth for a transformational experience.

Each book has a matching meditation audio available for your listening pleasure at http://www.togetherpublishing.com. Please visit our site for your gifts. The book and the audio have similar wording, yet according to the Archangels, they Upgrade us differently. Each medium has a unique experience, energetically Upgrading us in distinct ways. Each time you read or hear an Archangel Upgrade, a new dimension is added or adjusted for your benefit.

Become interactive with your book; when inspired, read the words aloud, and let them roll over you, feeling the love and magic that the Angels radiate. When inspired create your own rituals; there is no right or wrong way. As you play with the rock stars of the Celestial realm, you can expect your life to become more heavenly, more peaceful.

You may Notice Many Words are Uniquely Capitalized throughout this series; this is yet another way the Angels infuse us. When you see this try to feel that word or phrase; sensing the depth of its Intensity of Pure Divine Light throughout your Being.

The Archangel Energy is neither male nor female. This gender fluidity is made clear in this series by the use of the word they or she/he to convey a non-gender energy that shifts roles to uplift and nurture you. The upgrades happen in Divine Time, and there is no schedule. There is no competition. There is no rush. Wherever you are in the process is perfect.

A word about the length of this book. "Less is more." This Series of books is the result of decades of study in the art of Law of

Attraction, Angelic knowing and energy healing, condensed here for you in a format that will shift and benefit the reader. If you found your way here, you can expect miracles. As Einstein said, "There are only two ways to live your life. One is as though nothing is a miracle. The other is as though everything is a miracle." The matching audio to this book is 44 minutes, so working with that is always an option.

Both Neville Goddard and Albert Einstein stated that our imagination is the creative force. Goddard went so far as to imply that our imagination is the God/dess Energy. I mention this to you because as you read these words with much more than your eyes, let your imagination run wild with vivid pictures of the love the magical Archangels have for you and of your adventures together. Enjoy.

ABOUT ARCHANGEL MICHAEL

I'm so excited to introduce you to Archangel Michael! They are the Divine Archangel of Protection and Boundaries. In the Archangelology Series, they gift Us with protection and Love from the heavenly dimensions. Archangel Michael infuses us with a Loving strength that surrounds us with Protective Energies. This function of Michael's tools for guidance helps us to feel safe. Also, Michael cuts cords, or attachments, on our behalf from people, places, or things that no longer serve us. Michael aids us in releasing attachments formed in unproductive relationships. As we call on and work with Michael, we can expect our relationships to shift for the better or dissolve if they are no longer for our highest good. Michael equips us with Energetic Barriers of Love and Light that shield us from what we do not want. They remind us of the extent of Our power and allows us to take back responsibility for what is ours energetically. As in Michael assists in releasing baggage that is weighing us down. They do this all with the precision of a Samurai Light Master; Upgrading our innate abilities by building on beneficial energy practices we already possess. This Divine Knowledge may take some time to integrate, but the final result is well worth the wait. The culmination of your efforts comes to fruition in your transformation into a New Glorious Human aka Earth Angel. Michael helps to develop our imagination for the purpose of visualizing the people we love in a very safe place, thriving on their own. Releasing unproductive worrying can help center us and make us more peaceful beings. As you work with Michael, you can expect fundamental, positive shifts and feelings of peace and safety. Your experience with Michael is meant to be an interactive one, as you reacquaint yourself with this Divine Being and your power. Their guidance will help you shift your consciousness, making you a magnet for confidence, peace, and prosperity in new refreshed ways. Spending time with Archangels creates a heavenly life. The information I have put together is meant to work for your individualized wants and needs. It is not a prescribed set of general steps or rules, but rather it aims to help you in your particular journey and give you what you need to begin or grow in a mindset. You may read a sentence, a paragraph, or the whole book. It's just whatever you feel you need to embark on this Celestial journey to a more abundant life. There is no right or wrong way to use this tool. The only thing I recommend you keep in the forefront of your practice is to ensure you are enjoying the process. Meet one of the Archangels in the Archangelology Book and Audio Series that is here to help you at this time. If you call Archangel Michael, they will come, just as all of the Archangels will come to your assistance when beckoned. For gifts from the Archangels visit http://www.togetherpublishing.com.

ARCHANGEL MICHAEL

A rchangelology, Michael. Deep Healing Breaths. Let us ground, center and connect to the Divine energies present at all times. We are now going to spend some time with the beautiful, magnificent Archangel Michael. Visualize before you now Archangel Michael in all their, glory, beauty, stamina, bright white light, and brilliance. Archangel Michael radiates, carries and infuses us with the Divine Healing Blue Light Ray. Feel that delicious blue ray caressing your energy field now.

The Angel Energy is neither male nor

female, so just let this beautiful, knowing come to you, that Angels are all around you, that their energy is Divine and is a blend of the God/dess force with the female-male aspects.

Archangel Michael wants you to know that they have been watching you in a loving, mothering/fathering way and waiting with such patience for you to call them into your life. Angels have such, such Divine Patience.

Archangel Michael has the Divine gift and ability to cut cords. Now, of course, Michael has many, many abilities, yet Archangel's gift at cutting cords is what they want to share with you now. They want you to know that you can be as light and bright and free beyond anything you have imagined and your imagination is being activated now. Imagination is such an important skill in our lives, and the Archangels are helping us now to cultivate sweet imagination.

Take a deep healing breath. Sit back as comfortable as you can be. Archangel Michael wants you to get so cozy, and look up and gaze upon a screen, a beautiful panoramic screen so bright, so brilliant it looks completely real. Colors are so clear, so crisp that you can smell it and hear it and taste it on this Divine Screen. Standing up now, are you and Archangel Michael. Michael is standing before you now in all their brilliance. Beautiful, white expanded wings, glorious silver armor that fits like a glove, perfect in physique. This beautiful, Divine Being is looking upon you with such sweet Divine Love that you feel it in every cell of your body. You feel your Divinity. You feel how truly loved you are. You feel how blessed you are. You feel it like rays of blue ray light igniting all of your being, all that you are. Feel it. Feel that beautiful, beautiful love. Yes.

Just relax and float into this love. Relax and feel the sounds circling you, waving through you, enjoying such a healing, peaceful experience, and take a deep breath. Now, Archangel Michael telepathically answers that question you're having right now. You're asking, "Why me? Why would such a Divine, gorgeous being as Archangel Michael, who is more beautiful, more radiant, more light than any movie star I've ever seen, than any beautiful being, why would someone of that immense caliber have such deep Love and reverence for me now?" Archangel Michael stares deep into your eyes and lifts their beautiful hand and places it right in your heart chakra, and you feel such tingles and such waves of light and love that you can't even think. All you can do is feel. All you can do is feel this deep, sweet, Divine Love as Archangel merges with you now and gives you all the Love that you've ever desired, that you've always craved. Take a deep Breath. Feel this Love deep throughout every Cell in your mind-body and your spirit. In every atom and fiber of your being, feel Celestial Love now. Feel it waving through your body. Smile. Yes. Feel Archangel Michael's celestial Love filling you so deeply that you start to glow and levitate a bit and smile. Feel it. Yes. Look at the screen and see Michael's face, how they are looking at you with pure, sheer, sweet love, Yes, feel that Divine Source of love flowing into every cell in your body now. Feel the radiance, feel the infusion, feel the light. As you feel this, raise your hand with me now and repeat after me. Take a deep breath.

"Archangel Michael, please come into my life now and fill my life with deep, sweet Archangel Love, and cut all cords that bind me in any way. Cut all cords with any person, place, or thing that are no longer for my highest good. Archangel Michael, I ask you to do this. I ask the Divine Source of God/dess in you to quietly remind me, that you are doing all this for me out of your great Love for me, and it humbles me. Thank you, Archangel Michael, for this Divine, Divine gift that you are bestowing upon me that is my birthright. Thank you." Take a deep healing breath.

Michael wants to show you a gift that they have for you. They want to show you what they can do for you. Take a deep healing breath. Michael pulls out their beautiful, strong sword. See Michael standing in all their glory before you. Michael telepathically communicates to you now at this moment that this sword is for your protection, that Michael protects you in every moment in time-space, and anytime you need you can picture Michael standing there beside you, before you, behind you, any place you choose. With that strength, with their strong arms covered in muscles, arms gorgeous and strong, holding that beautiful sword of light. Now, see the light emanating from that sword, so bright, so clear, so silvery, so violety, so opalescent. The color changes at times. It's whatever you need at the moment, yet that sword is always beyond razor-sharp, and Michael is beyond a master at using the sword. They want to take care of you and protect you.

Now, Michael instills this knowledge deep within you so that you may always feel protected, safe, and guided by the Divine Intelligence and Divine Beings; and all you need do is surrender and let go. Take a deep breath.

Ask with me now: "I ask the Divine Energies to quiet, calm and lay my ego to rest. I ask the Divine Energies to reactivate my ability to think with my Heart. My Heart's thinking ability, yes." Take a deep, healing breath. Feel that radiating throughout every Cell in your body. Feel the Divine Love. Feel your Heart Thinking for you now. Ah, yes, the tingles. Smile. The Divine Intelligence of your Heart is in Charge now. In Charge of your mind and any words that you might say so that you may share your Angelic Voice. Take a deep breath.

Michael now works with you. They want you to set intentions for any cords that need cutting in your life. See yourself up on the screen. Michael shows you pictures. The Divine Intelligence shows what would help to be released now. Michael wants you to know that when we cut cords, it doesn't mean that we're going away from these people, places, or things. It means that we're clearing any energies from the person, situation, or thing that no longer serves us. Cutting cords is a Divine, Sweet Action. It is an action of Divine Intelligence, and we don't have to understand it. All we have to do is let it happen and get out of the way. Inhale. If things are for our highest good, they will stay. If things are not for our highest good, they will shift and either gently float away or change for the better.

Divine Intelligence is in Charge, yet Michael wants you to know that we even cut cords with the people we Love because we release all attachments. We set everyone and everything free, in that Clean, Clear space. See it. This way the beautiful, perfect things that our Hearts desire, truly want, can come to us. There's no need to cling to anything anymore. There never was. The veils and illusions are lifted, and our sweet Heart Thinking comes in. We surrender to the Divine Intelligence, to the Archangels and with blessings and great joy allow them to lead us, to walk beside us, behind us. Inhale. Activate our God/dess self.

Now, Archangel Michael wants you to think of any people that have been heavy on your mind. Archangel Michael puts a bubble of strong diamond light around that person and a bubble of strong diamond light around you, and you are grounded to the beautiful Goddess Mother Earth. As this happens with Mother Earth, beautiful Divine Gaia, feel your deep love for Gaia. Our Goddess, our mother who supplies us with all, feel it. That's how we get our Heart Centered. We feel that Love for our beautiful Earth, and we just radiate Love. Now, Archangel Michael gently, efficiently, with the knowing and intensity of a samurai master, cuts any cords between you and this person. Yes. Now watch them in their diamond light bubble as they gently float free from you. Ahhh, feel that. Yes, yes. Feel the tingles. Feel the freedom. Feel your third eye vibrating with White Violet Light as this happens.

Now exhale. Archangel Michael anchors this knowledge, and they will do this in one billionth of a second anytime you even think and ask them to do this for you. This is anchored for you now. This is one of your Angel abilities now. When I say Angel abilities, something beautiful happens. Your Earth Angel Wings pop right out. Smile. Yes, you are an Earth Angel. Now, feel the freedom and know that anytime you're thinking of someone and picture those diamond light bubbles, that sword, that release, and pop! It's done. You are Free. They are Free. Everyone is Free to float, to Love, to be free of fear, to float to the beautiful higher dimensions and Love. The Love and Light in these higher dimensions we create with our Hearts. We create on new beautiful levels in the higher dimensions. Yes, feel them as you float. Inhale. Exhale.

Now, look at your screen as Archangel Michael floats with you. Archangel Michael calls forth the institutions that you are going to clear and make peace with now. This could be a health system, it could be an educational institution, it could be a religious organization, it could be a corporate establishment or any institution. Take a deep healing breath. You are surrounded by a bubble of white diamond light. There is nothing to fear. See this whole institution in a bubble of White Diamond Light. Yes, you are that powerful. That whole gigantic organization, it could be government, it could be anything that feels heavy to you. See it in a bubble of White Diamond Light. Mm-hmm, beautiful light. Now watch Archangel Michael with the precision of a samurai master. They cut that cord, chop. Wow. Did you feel that? Feel the Relaxation and Peace from the Release. Yes, now Archangel Michael anchors that ability in. Yes, oh, feel it. Smile. It's, overwhelmingly beautiful.

Anytime you need that to happen, you

just think, and Archangel Michael has your back. They have got this for you. They are all powerful, they are all knowing, they are protection. They are the God/dess Energy for you. Yes. Deep healing breath. Inhale. Feel yourself floating higher with Michael. Feel the freedom. Ah, relax in it. Laugh. Feel the tingles. Ah yes, feel the brilliance. Feel your power. Feel what you've just done. You are an Earth Angel. Smile. Did you see your wings pop out again, your beautiful, etheric wings? See them. Focus your eyes and see yourself floating, flying, moving with Archangel Michael. Exhale. Yes, you are that Divine. You are that powerful. You are an Earth Angel floating. Feel it. Feel the Clouds around you. See the beautiful, brilliant sky. Ah, in the distance, see other Angels floating around in the Clouds. So many different Angels. Look around and see them all. See them shimmering, the lights, all there for you.

Archangel Michael and all the Archangels want you to know this and feel this. What a Divine, blessed being you are. How everything is being orchestrated with such Divine Intelligence. How everything you want is coming to you, and at the perfect moment, so there's no rush. You're in no competition. There's no need for fear or worry. You are on Divine Archangelic time now. Things here in the Celestials, things are unique. Things are a little different than what you have experienced before. There's more Ease, Joy, Flow, Support, Abundance, Well-Being, Wisdom, Knowing, and there's more Knowing that All is Well, that All Hath always been Well. There's the Divine Knowing, Divine Wisdom, that the Archangels have our back. Archangel Michael has your back. What a blessed, beautiful thing to know. Feel that throughout your Whole Body, that one of your Divine Friends is one of the Archangels. Feel that.

Now, Archangel Michael is calling your attention to anything to which you feel too attached. This could be an account or objects in the home that may be better to release to charity, to other people that need them. You and your Archangel will know what these attachments are. You will feel it. Archangel Michael helps you. Now, put that object and yourself in separate Diamond Light bubbles. Ground yourself, secured to the Divine, beautiful Mother Earth; see beautiful Mother Earth. Feel that love that's radiating from you now and say, "Michael, relBase me," and it just happened. With the precision of the Divine Intelligence, Michael cut that cord incredibly fast. Now, watch that thing float away and take a deep, healing breath. Ah, feel the freedom.

Do not worry about this thing. If it's meant to Be with you, it will, in a newly refreshed way, in a new powerful, Abundant way, in new ways that you have yet to imagine. If it is meant to leave, something better and higher will come in its place. We let our Heart do our thinking because the gifts that are waiting to be bestowed upon us are beyond anything that we have imagined yet today, and they are coming. Archangel Michael has another gift to bestow upon you. They are smiling because they are very excited about this gift and you're smiling because you feel what's coming. You know something wonderful is coming now to help you. Take a deep breath. Connect to your beautiful Gaia, to your Mother Earth. Yes, feel her. Feel all the Love Flowing through your Heart chakra. Yes, get in your Heart space as you see yourself up on the screen with Archangel Michael.

Archangel Michael now covers you in the most luminecient silvery suit. It is unique to you. Michael has their look. Your suit is an armor of diamond light. It has a beautiful, diamond shimmer, and it has a hard look too, a strong look to it. From the Angelic Realms, this material moves with you. It is covering you now. Deep healing breath. Inhale. You feel it. Yes, this suit, you look magnificent in this suit, and it covers your head too. You look fabulous. You see yourself, and you're smiling. Archangel Michael is going to anchor this suit in for you now. This suit protects you from anything unwanted. This suit keeps you safe. No negative energies can penetrate this suit. No implants that you do not prefer can permeate this suit. When you are in your suit, when you put the suit on, you are so safe and so protected with the brilliant, beautiful diamond white light.

Feel your suit now. Yes, feel how strong

you are. Archangel Michael wants you to be strong like them. Take a deep breath. Yes, feel the radiance of this suit. It shines like diamonds. It fits perfectly to your body. It's comfortable like skin. It's magic. It is yours now; it is anchored into your being for Wellness, Peace, Abundance, Joy, Bliss. Yes, deep healing breath. Now, if you like, you can see your Angel Wings sprout out. This is up to you. In this suit, you float. You feel peaceful. You feel relaxed. You know your power in your suit, and you can Activate it at any time you like. You relax knowing that you are home. Archangel Michael wants you to understand that with all these gifts and abilities that you are creating and that are being bestowed upon you through the Angelic Realm, you have the ability to place anyone that you like in this diamond light suit, in their personal, unique, beautiful suit.

You don't need to worry about anyone anymore. You can let these people go on their journey, on their path. Archangel instills in you the knowledge that worrying doesn't help them and it doesn't help you. We're human. Sometimes, it happens. It's okay. We are playing with the Angels now. We are surrendering to their Divine Intelligence and their Divine Guidance. Take a deep, healing breath. Let's play with our new skill. Connect with the beautiful Mother Earth. Feel her. Feel her Love radiating throughout you. Feel how much Mother Earth, the Goddess, does for us, how much she loves us, how much she supplies for us. Yes, feel it, as you start to smile. Watch yourself doing this up on the screen. Now, call on someone you Love about whose wellbeing you're a little concerned, that needs more health, more abundance, or protection. See them in front of you.

You may do this with as many beings as you like at any time you want. You are an Earth Angel now. See this being or beings in their suit, see how they smile. They're smiling, and they're looking down at their suit, their diamond, gorgeous looking suit. Take a deep healing breath with them. Now, as they're in their suit and they're so happy, and they're so safe, feel this with them now for a moment as you and they both are encapsulated in your healing bubble of white diamond light. Now you see them in their suit, and they're floating, floating away from you a bit, and this is fine. We're going to give them a little space, and I want you to see as a legion of Divine Angels surrounds this person, animal or being, whoever needs the help at the moment. All our sweet, sweet friends. Yes, and see them in their light suit, so happy and being taken care of by the beautiful Angelic beings, the Archangels, the masters of light. Take a deep healing breath.

See your beings, all of them, your family, your friends, someone you see even on the street that needs help, whoever you as an Earth Angel choose to do this for, and let go and know you don't have to do a thing. Archangel Michael and the legions of Archangels are taking care of this person now. Just let go of them. Yes, just do it. Take a deep, healing breath. Feel the freedom. Feel the release. Feel your third eye tingling with the great Divine Intelligence, knowing that non-attachment, that letting others go, is a brilliant piece of Angelic knowledge that you have now. Take a deep, healing breath.

Now, Archangel Michael wants to spend a little time with you, just the two of you together, and they want to fill up any of those places where they cut those cords, wherever they may be. They wants to fill them with shimmers of beautiful, opalescent rainbow light. Ah, yes. See the purple swirls, the blue ray, the deep-emerald greens, the brilliant yellows. See colors you've never seen before. Let them fill your aura. Let them fill any places where Michael released and cut. Let them fill your Heart deeply, feel their sparkles of light filling your third eye with shimmers of beautiful, violet light. Yes, feel it shimmering in your third eye. Ah, Peace. Take a deep, healing breath.

Feel blue shimmers at your throat chakra, healing and soothing you, letting you know it's safe to speak words of Love and Health. Yes, shimmering, sparkling. Feel the beautiful, shimmering at your base chakra, right at the base of your spine, of deep, delicious violet plum red. See that color glowing there. Right now, the base of your spine, yes. Shimmer, shimmer it there. Ah, yes. Deep breath. You feel it, then go to the area right where your belly button is. In that area, we're going to shimmer sweet, delicious yellow, a delicious lemon yellow. Archangel Michael is shimmering and filling that area with strong self-confidence, with deep knowing, of just how brilliant and smart and powerful you are. You are a beautiful, bright Earth Angel, and you bring such Love, such Divine sweet Love to this world, and you are so deserving of Love.

See that yellow sparkling; you are so deserving of everything you want, of everything you desire. Feel the infusion of deep Love in that area. Let it sink in. Feel your magnificence. Feel how marvelous you are. Smile. Feel how the Angels love you. See surrounding you now a brilliant team of Angels, pulsating you with Love and Light from the higher Celestial dimensions. Feel it. Take a deep breath. Right below the belly button between the base of your spine. We are going to see the sacral chakra as orange, and we're going to see it glowing and sparkling and grounding us with Prosperity. Yes, Michael shimmers prosperity on you now to your solar plexus and shimmers to you the knowing that you are connected to Divine Abundance. Everything you need is flowing to you at the moment; you no longer need to look to any person, place, or thing; you now look to the unseen realms of the Archangels, and these beautiful Angels float to you.

Everything you need in every moment, you are beyond deserving. You are beyond Blessed. Yes, now a beautiful white diamond light will start at the base of your chakras and will move Up, Up, Up, and out your head and shimmer over you like a fountain. This light can change colors, and the Angels will help you and guide you with the exact color you need. Deep healing breath. You are at this moment a beautiful, shimmering being of light. You are at this moment a Divine Earth Angel. You are connected to all your Angels. Thank you. Thank them. Archangel Michael blessed being of Divine Protection and Love. Yes. So be it, so be it.

4

ANGELIC MANIFESTATION
JOURNAL BONUS

Create more of the life you want with the Archangels as you explore and focus with your Angelic Journal. If you are ready, let's set intentions now to make your Archangel Michael Book a Manifestation tool. It is said that humans have so many thoughts going on in our heads at once that it is hard for Angels and Spirit Guides to hear what we want help with. This is one of the many reasons it is so powerful to get very clear on what we desire and write it out in a designated journal for our Archangels. This way, they can understand our needs better and help us with our dreams and goals in Divine Time.

It has been proven that when we write things down, more of what we desire comes to us. Goals get accomplished, and things flow with more ease. Adding the Amazing Archangels to your journaling just makes the results that much stronger. As we set intentions for what we want and take the time to focus and write it down in our journal, unseen forces move on our behalf. We are going to enlist the help of this Divine Knowing with our Archangel book in an interactive way and turn our book into a manifestation tool. We are also going to play with our books like children and have some fun. Children are powerful creators, and we will take on some of their great habits for their creative value.

Focus and underline ideas you resonate with in your book and become immersed in Upliftment. There is a deeper connection as we become interactive with our Archangel books. We may get colored pens and underline areas of our book that feel important or special to us. We may want to draw pictures of desired blessings or anything that makes us feel good. We may want to mark different areas of our book with hearts, stars, or Angel wings. Get sticky tab notes, a personal favorite, and stick them to your favorite pages you want to return to often. In your journal section, place a sticky tab on an area you want to let the Angels know to help you write in and as a personal reminder. Let your Angelic interaction and intuition guide you with what feels best. Neville Goddard and Albert Einstein both explained that our imagination is a creative force and can bring great blessings to our lives. We will bring our imagination fully into our process now. You may want to add stickers to enhance pages. Place a beautiful angel or magic looking card in your book as a bookmark. Get creative and give your book some personal character. Putting clover or flowers in your book to press and dry, adds some powerful nature magic to your process. Roses are a great choice as they have the highest vibration of any flower. You may give lovely flowers as an offering to your Archangels as well. Giving back is always a beneficial activity.

Everyone has magical abilities. Some of us know this, and some do not. My point is all these ideas are simple and will work for anyone who puts forth an effort and has the faith to relax and let go so the angels may do their work. Of course, anything we put out comes back to us, so we want to always include "for the highest good" in all requests.

In all my studies of magical herbs, cinnamon is found in many different traditions for enhancement of all things wanted and removing things not wanted. You may want to rub a dab of cinnamon mixed with a touch of olive oil on your journal in an intentional shape such as a heart for more love or the infinity symbol for more abundance. Then say to yourself, "I anoint my journal with success and happiness with the help of the Archangels." Anointment has been practiced for eons with much luck and advancement. Basil and Sage could just as easily be utilized. Anything that feels magical and speaks to you in your spice cabinet most likely has wonderful magical properties. Use these gifts of nature with intention and focus for a more joyous life. The idea is to create a magnet for all you desire that is for your highest good with your Archangel Journal.

You may want to underline ideas in colors that mean something to you. The sky is the limit, get creative and juicy with your book, knowing that amazing things are being created.

Next, we have dedicated pages that are waiting for you to fill them with your heart's desires that Michael will help you achieve as long as they are for the highest good. You may write anything you want in your Archangel Journal. There is no right or wrong way to do this. You may ask the Archangels to help you release things from your life, share your hopes and dreams, or ask questions. I ask my angels questions, patiently wait, and know they will lead me to the answer in Divine Time.

Be open and honest with your journaling and the Archangels understanding that the only ones who need to see your Angel Journal are you and your Angels. Keeping your wishes to yourself is very powerful for manifesting as well.

We have created categories for you, and

of course, there will Be freestyle areas, so play with this and have fun. After you play with your journal, you may put it away in a sacred space knowing all is in Divine Order. Remember, magic works just in its own time and asking where the results are will only block things, so relax, have faith, and patience. Keep this dream book; you will be pleasantly surprised when you check on it at later dates. You may come back to read your Michael book and add more to it at any time. Know that unseen beneficial forces are moving to help you now and forevermore. Play with and collect other Archangelology books and audios, remembering, "If you call them, they will come." Check out the Archangelology Archangel Journaling Book for more ideas on taking your Journaling Process to the next "celestial" level. The Archangels have tied this whole series Together for us in such a Divinely Intelligent way. Spend time in nature with your book, filling it with love, imagination, and Angelic magic for exponential results. You are a powerful creator and loved by all that is.

Write on the blank areas of your book

and on the lined journal areas. Think outside of the box and let your kid like creative energies flow. Have fun, and add your own flair.

Please enjoy the process and expect wonderful things.

WELL-BEING JOURNALING

I Am filled with Well-Being and Archangel Michael stands by my side anytime I call them. Write out all the Well-Being you are experiencing and any Divine Plans that come to mind for the highest good to manifest.

I AM CREATING SPACE FOR MORE VITALITY

RELATIONSHIP JOURNALING

I Am Aligning with more fulfilling relationships and Archangel Micheal has my back.

I FOCUS ON WIN-WIN RELATIONSHIPS

FINANCIAL BLESSINGS
JOURNALING

My financial goals are accomplished with the help of Archangel Michael.

I AM FORTUNATE

PERSONAL JOY JOURNALING

I AM attracting things that bring me joy and bliss with the help of Archangel Michael.

I AM LAUGHING AND HAVING FUN

THE FUN IS JUST BEGINNING

FREESTYLE JOURNALING FOR A
BLESSED LIFE

Fill these pages with any fun and unique ideas that you desire your Archangels to help you line Up with. Have fun. Get out your colored pens. Draw rainbows, baseballs, Angel wings and anything that makes you smile.

I AM LETTING MY CREATIVE
ENERGIES FLOW

JOURNALING FOR NEW PROJECTS

I deas for new projects my Archangels help me bring to Life for the highest good.

I AM A MASTER CREATOR

JOURNALING YOUR GRATITUDE

F ill these pages with the things you are truly grateful for. Let the Archangels and Divine Energy know how much you appreciate them. Draw pictures for them as gifts or press clovers or flowers here as offerings for all they do for you.

**I AM GRATEFUL FOR ALL THIS
AND MORE**

I AM GRATEFUL FOR THESE BLESSINGS

12

MY FAVORITE THINGS

Take time, get by yourself, and write a list of things you love to do. Write out things you love to think about that bring you peace, bliss, and Joy.

13

BLESSINGS

May the Divine Creative Force that Moves and Creates the Universes Bless and Enhance Every Wish You Ever Conceived that is for the Highest Good of All Involved. May Joy, Peace, and Purpose Be Yours all the Days of your Lives. Through All Time Space and Dimensions. So Mote it Be, and So It Is. I hope this book helps you in wonderful ways and radiates out to a gorgeous future for you and yours.

Kim

REFERENCES

~

Anna Merkaba. Mission To Earth: A Light workers guide to self mastery. (Merkaba Healing Inc.)

Chaudhary Sufian. World of Archangels: How to Meet an Archangel. (Sufian Chaudhary 2012).

Esther and Jerry Hicks. The Essential Law of Attraction Collection. (Hay House).

Matias Flury. Downloads From The Nine: Awaken As You Read. (Matias Flury 2014).

14

MORE OFFERINGS

~

Visit http://www.togetherpublishing.com to discover more Archangels and Super Power Saints

Each of the following books has a matching audio filled with healing music.

Archangelology Michael * Protection

Archangelology Raphael * Abundance

Archangelology Camael * Courage

Archangelology Gabriel * Hope

Archangelology Metatron * Well Being

Archangelology Uriel * Peace

Archangelology Haniel * Love

Archangelology Raziel * Wisdom

Archangelology Zadkiel * Forgiveness

Archangelology Jophiel * Glow

Archangelology Violet Flame * Oneness

Archangelology Sun Angels * Power

Archangelology Moon Angels *
Magnetism

Archangelology Sandalphon *
Harmony

Archangelology Orion * Expansion

The items below come in book only

Archangelology * Archangel Journaling

Archangelology * Archangel
Breath-Tap Book

How Green Smoothies Saved My
Life Book

Activate Your Abundance Book and Audio
Program

The rest of the items below are available in Audio Format

Archangelology * Breath-Tap Super Power Saints Volume 1 Audio

Archangelology * Breath-Tap Super Power Saints Volume 2 Audio

Regeneration Meditations * Switchword Series with Solfeggio Frequencies audio

Radiating Divine Love * Switchword Series with Solfeggio Frequencies audio

Love Charm * Switchword Series with Solfeggio Frequencies audio

Dragon Sun Grounding Meditations * Cosmic Consciousness Series audios

Sweet Moon Sleep Meditation * Cosmic Consciousness Series

Enchanted Earth Sacred Geometry * Cosmic Consciousness Series audios

SUPER POWER SAINTS BREATH-TAP AUDIOS

M eet the Super Power Saints
Available now at
https://togetherpublishing.com

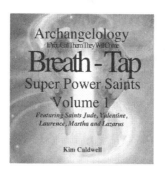

BE AN ANGEL

If you enjoyed this book or received any help from it please give it a positive review so others may find it as well. Thank you so much for your time.

Kim